MW01124921

American Indian Nations

The Chumash

Seafarers of the Pacific Coast

by Karen Bush Gibson

Capstone press
Mankato, Minnesota

Capstone Press
151 Good Counsel Drive, P.O. Box 669, Mankato, Minnesota 56002
www.capstonepress.com

Library of Congress Cataloging-in-Publication Data
Gibson, Karen Bush.
    The Chumash Indians: seafarers of the Pacific coast / by Karen Bush
Gibson.
        p.cm.—(American Indian nations)
        Includes bibliographical references and index.
        ISBN 0-7368-2179-1 (hardcover)
        1. Chumash Indians—Juvenile literature. [1. Chumash Indians.
2. Indians of North America—California.] I. Title. II. Series.
E99.C815G52 2004
979.4004'9757—dc21   2002156007

Summary: Provides an overview of the past and present lives of the
Chumash people, tracing their customs, family life, history, culture, and
relations with the United States.

Editorial Credits

Blake A. Hoena and Charles Pederson, editors; Kia Adams, series designer;
Molly Nei, book designer and illustrator; Kelly Garvin, photo researcher;
Karen Risch, product planning editor

Photo Credits
cover images: Chumash 'ap, Marilyn "Angel" Wynn;
Chumash basket, Lillian Smith

Capstone Press/Gary Sundermeyer, 17
Corbis/Tom Bean, 7; David Muench, 15
Getty Images/Hulton Archive, 26
North Wind Picture Archives, 28, 30
PhotoDisc Inc, 16–17
Raymond Bial, 4–5, 20–21, 36–37
San Diego Historical Society, 24
Santa Barbara Historical Society, 32–33
Santa Barbara Museum of Natural History, 14, 19, 38, 40, 43;
    Mike Ward, 12; Peter Howorth, 18; Stanley Edwards, 23; Daily
Nexus, Genevieve Field (1989), 34; Lillian Smith, 45
Santa Ynez Valley Historical Society, 8–9

**Capstone Press thanks anthropologist Jan Timbrook for her help
in producing this book.**

2 3 4 5 6 08 07 06 05 04

Table of Contents

1 Who Are the Chumash? 5
2 The Early Chumash 9
3 Change Comes to the Chumash 25
4 The Chumash Today 35
5 Preserving Chumash Ways 41

Features

Map: The Chumash Past and Present . . . 11
Recipe: Acorn Pancakes 17
Chumash Timeline 44
Glossary 46
Internet Sites 46
Places to Write and Visit 47
For Further Reading 47
Index 48

Modern Chumash live much like other Americans.

Chapter One

Who Are the Chumash?

Scientists believe that Chumash Indians are descendants of ancient people who lived in southern California thousands of years ago. The Chumash were once a seafaring people living along the coast and on the islands in the area. Today, most Chumash live on the Santa Ynez Reservation or in nearby California towns. The 2000 U.S. Census counted 4,032 people as Chumash.

The name "Chumash" means "bead money makers." Originally, native people on the mainland in southern California gave this name to people living on islands in the area. The island people made money from certain shells. Later, the name "Chumash" came to include the native people living on the mainland as well.

Southern California offered a good life to early Chumash. They experienced mild, rainy winters and warm, dry summers. They had fresh water from nearby streams and rivers. The Chumash gathered fruits, seeds, and plant roots to eat. The ocean provided them with many kinds of fish and shellfish. The Chumash also hunted game animals in wooded and grassland areas.

Spanish explorers, missionaries, and settlers had a great influence on the Chumash. In 1542, the Spanish sailed north from Mexico. They were the first Europeans to meet the Chumash. The Spanish saw many Chumash villages near the ocean and on the Channel Islands. The Spanish created religious settlements called missions and taught Christianity to the Chumash. The Chumash also learned the Spanish language. Even today, many Chumash speak Spanish.

Modern Chumash have many jobs. Most Chumash men and women work in Santa Barbara, San Luis Obispo, and Ventura Counties in California. They work as teachers, health care workers, construction workers, or as other professionals. Some Chumash work as archaeologists. These scientists learn about past cultures by studying items that people used long ago.

Today, the Chumash way of life is much different than that of their ancestors, but they still have great respect for nature. The Chumash believe that people depend on the things that come from the earth. The Chumash also believe people must respect and value nature.

A memorial on San Miguel Island honors Juan Rodríguez Cabrillo. He was the first European explorer to meet the Chumash Indians.

Some Chumash lived in villages in the mountains of southern California.

Chapter Two

The Early Chumash

No one knows exactly when the earliest people came to the southern coast of present-day California. Archaeologists have discovered signs that people lived in the area about 13,000 years ago. These early people may be ancestors of the Chumash.

Archaeologists believe the Chumash culture began about 3,000 years ago. The Chumash were made up of related groups of people who lived in south-central California. Similarities in languages and traditions linked these groups.

Groups of Chumash lived from present-day Malibu to Paso Robles. Some Chumash lived in the mountains to the east. Others lived on the Channel Islands. The largest number of Chumash lived on the coast near the Santa Barbara Channel.

Villages

No one person ruled over all the Chumash. Instead, each village had at least one chief. Chiefs led the villages, settled arguments, and saw that everyone had enough food to eat. The position of chief usually was passed down from father to son, but some chiefs were women.

Chumash villages ranged in size from fewer than 100 to more than 1,000 people. In large villages, houses stood in rows along pathways. Most villages included homes, storehouses, a dance ground, and a playing field for games. Each village also had a cemetery nearby.

A Chumash home was called an 'ap. These dome-shaped homes were made of willow poles and covered with reeds. A hole in the top allowed air to circulate and smoke from cooking fires to escape. A typical single-family 'ap was about

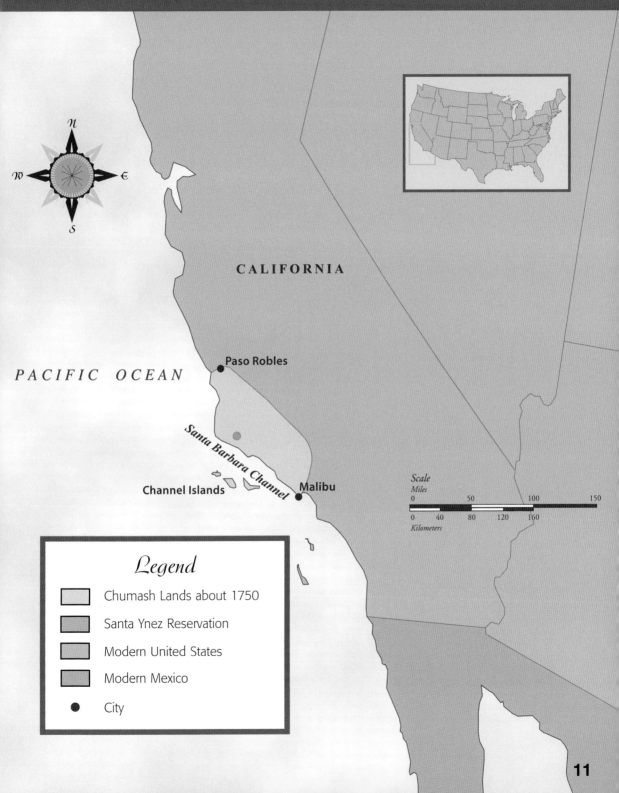

CALIFORNIA

PACIFIC OCEAN

Paso Robles

Santa Barbara Channel

Channel Islands

Malibu

Scale
Miles
0   50   100   150
0   40   80   120   160
Kilometers

Legend

- Chumash Lands about 1750
- Santa Ynez Reservation
- Modern United States
- Modern Mexico
- • City

12 to 20 feet (3.7 to 6.1 meters) wide. A chief's 'ap might be 35 feet (11 meters) wide. It was large enough to house some of his relatives.

Extended family members often lived together in one 'ap. After a couple married, they usually lived with the wife's family. Children grew up with their mother's relatives. Two or three related families often lived in one 'ap.

Chumash lived in dome-shaped homes made of willow poles covered with reeds.

Each village had at least one sweat lodge, called an 'apa'yik or temescal. An 'apa'yik was built partially underground. Mud covered the roof to hold in heat from a fire that was built inside. The men entered the 'apa'yik and sweated in the heat to cleanse their minds and bodies. At the end of the sweat, the men jumped in the ocean or a river. Men who were going hunting would put strong-smelling leaves on the fire in the sweat lodge. They stood in the fire's smoke so it would cover their human scent.

Spiritual Life

The spiritual leaders of the Chumash were called shamans. Shamans acted as a link between the Chumash and the spirits they believed in. Shamans used songs, prayers, and secret practices like rock painting to communicate with spirits.

Shamans had many duties. Shamans named children. They explained the meaning of people's dreams and other visions. They also foretold the future. Some shamans acted as doctors, using prayers, songs, and natural medicines to heal people's illnesses.

Ceremonies were important to Chumash spiritual life. Several times a year, Chumash from many villages had large ceremonial gatherings. They held ceremonies to honor

Hutash, or the Earth. The Chumash believed that she was the mother of their people. She filled the world with wild plants, game animals, and fish. The Chumash also honored Kakunupmawa, or the Sun. He brought warmth and light. In mid-winter, the Chumash held the Winter Solstice Ceremony. It included rituals to persuade the Sun to change directions and rise high in the sky to warm the Earth so plants could grow.

swordfish headdress

The Chumash performed dances during ceremonies. Many Chumash dances honored animals. The Chumash performed dances for foxes, blackbirds, bears, and coyotes. One important dance was the swordfish dance. The Chumash believed the swordfish was the chief of sea animals. The swordfish dancer wore a decorated swordfish skull. The Chumash offered beads and other gifts of thanks to the swordfish. They believed that the swordfish chased whales up onto beaches, providing meat to eat and bones for making tools and homes.

A religious society called 'antap played an important role in ceremonies. 'Antap members performed ceremonies and dances to keep balance in the world. The Chumash believed that people were responsible for balancing forces in the world that could help or harm nature.

Rock Art

Chumash shamans painted colorful images in caves and on rocks. They usually painted these images in special places far from villages. Rock paintings had spiritual meaning to the Chumash. They may have believed shamans used rock paintings to communicate with spirits.

The Chumash created paint and brushes from nature. They used an iron substance in rocks to make red and yellow colors. Black came from charcoal. White came from white clay or a mineral called gypsum. The colors were mixed with water, animal fat, or plant oil to form paint. For brushes, shamans used animal tails, plant fibers, or their fingers.

Most Chumash rock paintings are probably less than 1,000 years old, but some may be as old as 3,000 years. Examples of rock art include circles or stars inside other shapes. Some include figures that represent animals and people.

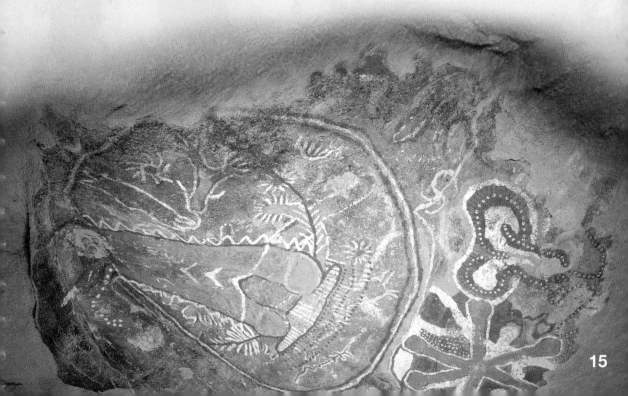

Food

The land and ocean provided the Chumash with food. Men and boys hunted deer and trapped small game animals, such as rabbits. Women and girls gathered acorns, pine nuts, and seeds from a plant called chia.

Food from the ocean was a large part of the Chumash diet. Archaeologists know this by studying hills of empty seashells near old village sites. Some of these shell hills are 30 feet (9 meters) high and about 1,450 feet (440 meters) wide. The Chumash ate clams, abalone, and mussels. They used the shells to make tools and jewelry.

Island and coastal Chumash hunted sea animals, caught fish, and gathered shellfish. Along the coasts, hunters crept up on seals and sea lions, using clubs to kill the animals. Fishers used spears called harpoons to hunt large fish, sea otters, and porpoises. They also used a net or a hook-and-line to catch fish. In streams, the Chumash used roots from the soap plant for fishing. Mashed soap plant roots dropped in water stopped fish from breathing. When the fish rose to the surface, people caught them by hand.

Acorn Pancakes

Acorns provided an important plant food for the Chumash. Acorns have a bitter taste and need to be prepared carefully. Chumash women pounded the acorns into powder. They removed the bitterness by pouring water through the acorn flour. Prepared acorn flour is used for this modern acorn pancake recipe.

Ingredients

⅔ cup (160 mL) acorn flour
(found in health food stores
or Asian markets)
⅓ cup (80 mL) all-purpose flour
1 teaspoon (5 mL) baking powder
¼ teaspoon (1.2 mL) salt
¾ cup (175 mL) milk

1 egg, beaten
2 tablespoons (30 mL) vegetable
oil
2 tablespoons (30 mL) honey or
maple syrup
1 tablespoon (15 mL) vegetable oil
honey or maple syrup for topping

Equipment

dry-ingredient measuring cups
liquid measuring cups
measuring spoons

medium mixing bowl
wooden mixing spoon
large frying pan

What You Do

1. Mix acorn flour, all-purpose flour, baking powder, and salt in medium bowl.
2. Add milk, egg, 2 tablespoons (30 mL) vegetable oil, and honey to mixture. Stir until thoroughly moistened.
3. Pour 1 tablespoon (15 mL) vegetable oil into large frying pan. Heat over medium heat.
4. Pour batter into the frying pan in ⅓-cup amounts. Cook until bubbles start to rise to surface. Then flip cakes and cook for 1 minute more. Repeat with remaining batter.
5. Top with honey or maple syrup and serve.

Makes about 6 pancakes

Tomols

The Chumash were excellent sea travelers and probably the finest native boatmakers in California. About 2,000 years ago, the Chumash began using plank canoes called tomols. The canoes helped them make trips between islands along the coast. The canoes made it easier for them to trade with other Chumash and to visit relatives in other villages. The Chumash also used tomols for fishing and for hunting seals, sea otters, and sea lions.

Tomols were made from redwood logs that the Chumash found as driftwood. Using stone tools, the Chumash split the logs into long planks. They shaped the planks with sharp stones and sanded them with sharkskin. After shaping the planks, the Chumash glued the planks edge to edge with pine sap mixed with natural tar. String made from plant fibers was used to tie the planks together. Lastly, the tomols were painted and decorated. The Chumash shaped two or three long paddles for each canoe. Tomols were between 12 and 30 feet (3.7 and 9.1 meters) long. Today, some Chumash make canoes similar to their ancestors.

Trade and Money

The Chumash traded among themselves and with neighboring American Indians. A large trading network was in place before A.D. 1200. Inland villages were trading centers between coastal Chumash and other Indians.

One type of trade was barter. The Chumash traded food items, shells, and animal skins for tobacco, jewelry, beads, and other goods. Chumash goods have been found as far east as Arizona.

Along with barter items, the Chumash traded using money made from seashells. More than 1,000 years ago, island Chumash were making olivella seashells into beads. The shells were cut into small pieces and a tiny hole was drilled into each one. The pieces were then polished until each bead was round and smooth. Different numbers of beads were placed on a

bead money

19

string to represent different amounts of wealth. The bead
strings were used as money for trading. With bead money, the

Chumash boys played a game with a hoop and spear, similar to the
ones pictured above, to practice their hunting skills.

Chumash could also pay for the services of doctors, dancers, and canoe makers.

Games

The Chumash loved gambling games. The Chumash believed supernatural forces caused people to win or lose. They bet bead money or other possessions. Gambling sometimes decided who might serve in a political position.

Boys and girls enjoyed shinny, peon, and other games. Shinny was a stickball game similar to field hockey. In peon, players guessed which hand held a colored bone. A hoop-and-pole game helped boys develop hunting skills. One boy rolled a hoop made from a branch that was bent and tied in a circle. Another boy tried to throw a spear through the hoop.

Chumash Beliefs

The Chumash believed the universe was divided into three layers. The top layer was the sky. It was the home of spirits called sky people. Some of the sky people were the Sun, the Moon, and the Morning Star. Chumash believed the Sun crossed the sky each day, carrying a torch made of burning cottonwood bark.

Humans lived in the middle level, called Earth. One ancient Chumash story says two giant snakes lived in the bottom layer and held up Earth. The snakes caused earthquakes whenever they moved.

Dangerous creatures called nunashish also lived in the lowest level. The Chumash believed these creatures sneaked up to the middle level at night to harm people.

Arts and Clothing

Many Chumash became highly skilled artists. They made shell and stone jewelry, bowls, and pipes. They decorated some of these items with carved designs or shell beads.

Chumash basket makers were especially famous. Even today, Chumash baskets are considered beautiful works of art. Some baskets were so tightly woven that they could hold water. Others were used to carry seeds, store food, and hold valuables. The Chumash used special cradle baskets to carry babies.

The Chumash did not wear much clothing. Children often wore nothing at all. Older girls and women usually wore a skirt made of leather or woven plant fibers. Women sometimes wore small basketry caps. Men often wore nothing except a belt for carrying tools. Chiefs might wear ankle-length capes of bearskin to show that they were important. In cool winter weather, the Chumash wore animal skins for warmth.

The Chumash often decorated themselves with paint and jewelry. At large gatherings, a painted design on a person's body represented the village where the person lived. People wore necklaces and earrings. All Chumash had pierced ears. Some pierced their noses. Most men had long hair tied up and decorated with pieces of wood, bone, or stone.

Chumash used stone bowls to grind acorns into flour. They used baskets to store food.

Juan Rodríguez Cabrillo was the first European to meet the Chumash Indians.

Chapter Three

Change Comes to the Chumash

The first Europeans to meet the Chumash were Spanish. In the early 1500s, Spanish explorers traveled north from Mexico. They were looking for places to set up settlements. On October 10, 1542, Juan Rodríguez Cabrillo sailed into the Santa Barbara Channel with a fleet of ships. Chumash in canoes came out to greet Cabrillo. The Spanish discovered that the friendly Chumash were eager to trade. The Chumash wanted to show the visitors their mainland and their island villages.

Spanish explorers had contact with the Chumash three more times between the late 1500s and early 1600s. Other meetings between the Spanish and Chumash probably occurred, but they were not recorded.

During the 1700s, Russians sailed south from Alaska to California. They were interested in killing seals and other animals for their fur. The Spanish wanted to claim the area and did not want Russians settling there. In August 1769, a group of Spanish soldiers and priests arrived in Chumash territory. They looked for the best places to build Spanish settlements. The Santa Barbara coast had plenty of wood,

The Spanish built presidios, or forts, in southern and central California to protect the area.

water, and pasture land for livestock. The Spanish decided to settle there. In 1782, the Spanish built a presidio, or military fort, in Santa Barbara to protect their interest in Chumash lands from the Russians.

About 22,000 Chumash lived in the area at the time. The Spanish wanted the Chumash to become Spanish citizens, follow the Roman Catholic religion, and obey Spanish laws.

The Mission Period

The mission period of Chumash history had already begun in 1772. That year, the Spanish built their first mission in Chumash territory. It was called Mission San Luis Obispo de Tolosa. Four other missions were built during the next 30 years. The Catholic priests at the missions successfully brought many Chumash to live in the missions and taught them the Christian religion.

At the missions, the Chumash traditional way of life was slowly replaced by European ways. Many Chumash became Catholics. The Chumash learned carpentry, tile making, farming, weaving, and pottery making. They depended on the missions for work and food. They learned to speak Spanish along with their Chumash languages.

The Chumash had a regular work schedule. They began work a little after sunrise and worked until the afternoon. Every few weeks, the priests allowed the workers to visit their relatives who still lived in villages.

A tragic effect of the mission system was the spread of diseases. The Spanish unintentionally carried deadly diseases

American Indians worked at Spanish missions.

Luhui

One very important woman leader among the Chumash was Luhui. She was born in the town of Liyam, the capital of the Santa Cruz Islands.

Luhui's father, Chief Suluwasunaitset, ruled over the Santa Cruz Islands. Before Luhui was born, a shaman went to the chief and his wife. The shaman said that their child would become ruler of the islands.

When Suluwasunaitset grew old, it was time to choose a new chief. Ordinarily, the chief's son would become the new chief. But Suluwasunaitset's only child was a daughter, Luhui. Some island Chumash did not want a woman to be chief. The Chumash fought over Luhui's right to be chief. Many people died.

The shaman went to the people and asked them to give up fighting. Eventually, the Chumash agreed that Luhui would be chief. Peace then returned to the islands.

to the Chumash. Nearly half the Chumash died within 13 years of entering the missions. One of the worst diseases was measles. The Chumash's bodies could not fight the measles germs. In 1806, hundreds of Chumash died from this disease.

The End of the Mission Period

In 1810, Mexico declared its independence from Spain. A long war followed. Mexico won its independence in 1821.

California became a Mexican state. Spanish control of the Chumash ended and Mexico assumed responsibility for the missions.

During the long battle for Mexican independence, the missions had not received enough supplies from the government in Mexico. The Chumash also were treated poorly. In 1824, many Chumash rebelled after a Mexican

The Santa Barbara Mission in California is still used for Roman Catholic services and ceremonies.

soldier beat a Chumash man at one mission. Fighting occurred at two other missions. Mexican soldiers stopped the rebellion.

By 1834, the Mexican government had given away much of the Chumash land and turned the missions over to private landowners. The Chumash had to leave the missions, but barely 1,000 Chumash were left. Many Chumash found work as household servants or cowboys on large ranches. A few returned to a more traditional way of life in villages far from the coast.

U.S. Influence

In the early to mid-1800s, Americans began settling in California. In 1848, the United States defeated Mexico in the Mexican War (1846–1848). Chumash land then passed from Mexican to U.S. control. In 1850, California became the 31st state.

California laws did not protect American Indian rights. As settlers moved to California, they moved onto Chumash homelands. By 1852, fewer than 600 Chumash existed. By 1880, the Chumash population had dropped to about 300.

In the late 1800s, the U.S. government began placing California Indians on reservations. The Chumash were one of the last California Indian nations to get their own reservation. On December 27, 1901, they were granted former church lands along Zanja de Cota Creek near the Santa Ynez Mission. Chumash had lived in this same area for many generations. The area was named the Santa Ynez Reservation.

Modern Chumash

Today, more than 150 Chumash live on the Santa Ynez Reservation. The reservation of 128 acres (52 hectares) is located 32 miles (51 kilometers) north of Santa Barbara, California.

Many different Chumash groups live in California. The Tejon Indian community near Bakersfield is made up of several tribes. Some of these people are descendants of Chumash who left their coastal homes during rebellions against the Spanish. Island Chumash joined other Chumash groups after the mission period ended. Some Chumash, like the San Luis Obispo band, are

identified by the mission where their ancestors lived. Other groups, including the Ventureño and Barbareño Chumash, are seeking federal recognition as Indian tribes. Currently, the U.S. government recognizes only the Santa Ynez band of Chumash.

Two Chumash Indians pose near the Santa Barbara Mission in southern California during the late 1800s.

Chumash celebrate their culture by performing traditional-style dances like the bear dance.

Chapter Four

The Chumash Today

Today, some Chumash live on the Santa Ynez Reservation, but most live in cities and towns in southern California. Some experts believe about 3,000 people of Chumash background live in Santa Barbara, San Luis Obispo, and Ventura Counties in California.

The Chumash live much like other Americans. They have modern housing. They hold the same kinds of jobs as other people.

A constitution and elected officials govern the Santa Ynez Reservation. People on the reservation who are 18 years old or older elect officers and vote on issues related to tribal money. A business committee oversees day-to-day tribal operations. Elections are held every two years to choose four committee members and a tribal chairperson. An elders council oversees cultural traditions and advises the business committee on cultural matters.

Like several other American Indian nations, the Santa Ynez Chumash opened a gambling casino. The casino is one of the largest employers in Santa Barbara County. The money earned at the casino pays for education and housing programs. Every registered member of the reservation gets a share of the casino's income. The tribe also donates money to organizations and community events outside the reservation.

The Chumash are concerned about other people and the environment. The Tribal Health Clinic serves Chumash and other people. The Santa Ynez Chumash run an environmental office that protects air, land, water, and cultural resources.

Religion is still important to the Chumash. Many Chumash are Roman Catholics. They follow the religion Spanish priests and missionaries brought to California. Some Chumash follow their traditional beliefs. Others have

Tribal government officials meet at the tribal office to discuss reservation issues.

combined parts of their traditional beliefs with Christian beliefs and what they have learned from other tribes. The Chumash still honor the natural world and all it provides.

Education is important to the Santa Ynez Chumash. The tribe provides scholarships for students who want to attend a college or a university. The Santa Ynez Chumash have one of the largest percentages of California Indians attending college.

Kitsepawit is a Chumash historical figure who helped preserve many of his people's traditions.

Kitsepawit (Fernando Librado)

Kitsepawit was born in 1839 to a Chumash family who had lived on Limuw, now called Santa Cruz Island. The Limuw islanders had already moved to the San Buenaventura Mission before Kitsepawit was born.

Kitsepawit spent his childhood at the mission. There, he learned Spanish, as well as the language of the Ventura Chumash. The priests at the mission baptized Kitsepawit and gave him the Spanish name Bernardo. But Chumash languages do not have "B" or "R" sounds, so Bernardo became known as Fernando, which was easier for the Chumash to say. The priests only gave Indians one name, but Kitsepawit eventually adopted the last name Librado.

Kitsepawit learned as much as he could about his Chumash background. When he was still a young boy, Kitsepawit watched Chumash men building plank canoes. In his middle years, Kitsepawit worked as a shepherd and ranch worker. He visited Chumash families working on nearby ranches. He learned the songs, dances, crafts, and stories of his people.

In his later life, Kitsepawit became friends with John Harrington. Harrington was an anthropologist. He studied people, cultures, and languages. Kitsepawit shared his knowledge of Chumash languages and culture with Harrington. Harrington took thousands of pages of notes on Kitsepawit's knowledge. Kitsepawit died in 1915, but scholars still use the information he provided to learn about the Chumash.

People preserve the Chumash culture by creating displays that show the traditional Chumash way of life.

Chapter Five

Preserving Chumash Ways

The Chumash are working hard to preserve their culture. They continue to pass it on through traditions like storytelling. Some Chumash work as archaeologists to study ancient Chumash objects. The Santa Barbara Museum of Natural History helps preserve Chumash history.

Laws have been passed to help the Chumash and other American Indians preserve their ways. For many years, Chumash items found at archaeological sites were taken by private collectors or put in museums. In the 1970s and 1980s, new laws were passed to protect Chumash cemeteries and historical sites. The Chumash now oversee any construction projects that affect sites where their ancestors once lived. Chumash also have a representative on the California Native Heritage Commission. This group works to protect the rights of California Indians and their cultures.

Some modern Chumash work to revive the Chumash languages. Language scholars have prepared dictionaries of Chumash languages. The University of California at Berkeley has workshops to teach Chumash about their languages. More people are studying Chumash all the time.

The Chumash culture teaches that all living things deserve respect. It teaches that people are responsible for keeping the natural world in balance. Today's Chumash face the pressures of modern-day life, but they try to live up to the responsibilities their ancestors taught. They are proud to continue their spiritual life and cultural traditions.

Oral Tradition

The Chumash have a history of storytelling, or oral tradition. They told stories for entertainment and to teach lessons to children. As with many tribes, the Chumash passed down stories from generation to generation.

Today, modern Chumash work to preserve their languages and traditions. Kitsepawit passed on many Chumash traditions and stories. Storyteller Vincent Tumamait (pictured below) was a Chumash elder who performed many Chumash stories. Other Chumash storytellers also continue to pass on the cultural traditions of their ancestors.

Chumash Timeline

Experts believe that people speaking a Chumash language were living in the Santa Barbara area around this time.

Spanish begin to set up missions on Chumash lands.

3000 B.C.   **A.D. 1542**   **1772**   **1821**

Juan Rodríguez Cabrillo makes first European contact with the Chumash.

California becomes a Mexican state when Mexico wins its independence from Spain; Mexican government takes control of the missions.

Chumash basket

Chumash rebellion occurs at three missions. Mexican soldiers stop the rebellion.

U.S. government sets up Santa Ynez Reservation.

1824   **1848**   **1901**   **1970s**

The United States defeats Mexico in the Mexican War and takes control of Chumash lands.

U.S. government passes laws to protect Chumash cultural and religious sites.

Glossary

'ap (AHP)—a Chumash home

'apa'yik (ah-pa-YIK)—a Chumash sweat lodge

archaeologist (ar-kee-OL-uh-jist)—a scientist who studies how people lived in the past

mission (MISH-uhn)—a religious settlement built by Spanish priests

reservation (rez-ur-VAY-shuhn)—land that the U.S. government set aside for American Indian tribes to use

shaman (SHA-muhn)—a religious leader

Internet Sites

Do you want to find out more about the Chumash? Let FactHound, our fact-finding hound dog, do the research for you.

Here's how:
1) Visit *http://www.facthound.com*
2) Type in the **Book ID** number:
   0736821791
3) Click on **FETCH IT**.

FactHound will fetch Internet sites picked by our editors just for you!

Places to Write and Visit

Chumash Interpretive Center
3290 Lang Ranch Parkway
Thousand Oaks, CA 91362

Santa Barbara Museum of Natural History
2559 Puesta del Sol Road
Santa Barbara, CA 93105

Santa Ynez Chumash
P.O. Box 517
Santa Ynez, CA 93460

For Further Reading

Heinrichs, Ann. *The California Missions.* We the People. Minneapolis: Compass Point Books, 2002.

Margaret, Amy. *Mission Santa Bárbara.* The Missions of California. New York: PowerKids Press, 2000.

McCall, Lynne, and Rosalind Perry. *California's Chumash Indians.* A Project of the Santa Barbara Museum of Natural History Education Center. San Luis Obispo, Calif.: EZ Nature Books, 2002.

Index

'antap, 14
'apa'yik, 13

baskets, 22, 23
bead money, 5–6, 19–21

Cabrillo, Juan Rodríguez, 7, 24, 25
California Native Heritage Commission, 42
canoe, 18, 21, 25, 39
casino, 36
ceremonies, 13–14, 30
chief, 10, 12, 23, 29
clothing, 22–23

dances, 14, 34, 39
disease, 28–29

education, 36, 38, 43

farming, 27
fishing, 6, 16, 18
food, 6, 10, 14, 16, 17, 19, 22, 23, 27
forts, 26, 27

games, 10, 20, 21

homes, 10, 12, 14, 35
'ap, 10, 12
hunting, 6, 13, 16, 18, 20, 21

island, 5, 6, 7, 18, 29
Channel Islands, 6, 10
Santa Cruz Island, 29, 39

jewelry, 16, 19, 22, 23

Kitsepawit, 38, 39, 43

language, 9
Chumash, 27, 39, 42
Spanish, 6, 27, 39
Librado, Fernando. See Kitsepawit

Mexico, 6, 25, 29–31
missions, 6, 27–28, 29, 30–31, 32
Mission San Luis Obispo de Tolosa, 27, 33
San Buenaventura Mission, 39
Santa Barbara Mission, 30, 33
Santa Ynez Mission, 32

population, 5, 27, 29, 31, 32, 35
of villages, 10

religion, 6
Christianity, 6, 27, 30, 37–38
traditional beliefs, 13, 15, 22, 37–38
rock painting, 13, 15

Santa Barbara Channel, 10, 25
Santa Barbara Museum of Natural History, 41
Santa Ynez Reservation, 5, 32, 35, 36, 37
shaman, 13, 15, 29
as doctors, 13, 21
storytelling, 41, 43
sweat lodge. See 'apa'yik

tomols, 18. See also canoes
tools, 14, 16
trade, 18, 19–21, 25

village, 6, 8, 10, 13, 15, 16, 18, 19, 23, 25, 28, 31